The clergyman's office, and the clergyman's due a sermon preach'd at the Triennial Visitation of the Right Reverend Father in God Edward, Lord Bishop of Gloucester at Campden, Octob. 7, 1698 / by Robert Morse ... (1699)

Robert Morse

Early English Books Online (EEBO) Editions

Imagine holding history in your hands.

Now you can. Digitally preserved and previously accessible only through libraries as Early English Books Online, this rare material is now available in single print editions. Thousands of books written between 1475 and 1700 and ranging from religion to astronomy, medicine to music, can be delivered to your doorstep in individual volumes of high-quality historical reproductions.

We have been compiling these historic treasures for more than 70 years. Long before such a thing as "digital" even existed, ProQuest founder Eugene Power began the noble task of preserving the British Museum's collection on microfilm. He then sought out other rare and endangered titles, providing unparalleled access to these works and collaborating with the world's top academic institutions to make them widely available for the first time. This project furthers that original vision.

These texts have now made the full journey -- from their original printing-press versions available only in rare-book rooms to online library access to new single volumes made possible by the partnership between artifact preservation and modern printing technology. A portion of the proceeds from every book sold supports the libraries and institutions that made this collection possible, and that still work to preserve these invaluable treasures passed down through time.

This is history, traveling through time since the dawn of printing to your own personal library.

Initial Proquest EEBO Print Editions collections include:

Early Literature

This comprehensive collection begins with the famous Elizabethan Era that saw such literary giants as Chaucer, Shakespeare and Marlowe, as well as the introduction of the sonnet. Traveling through Jacobean and Restoration literature, the highlight of this series is the Pollard and Redgrave 1475-1640 selection of the rarest works from the English Renaissance.

Early Documents of World History

This collection combines early English perspectives on world history with documentation of Parliament records, royal decrees and military documents that reveal the delicate balance of Church and State in early English government. For social historians, almanacs and calendars offer insight into daily life of common citizens. This exhaustively complete series presents a thorough picture of history through the English Civil War.

Historical Almanacs

Historically, almanacs served a variety of purposes from the more practical, such as planting and harvesting crops and plotting nautical routes, to predicting the future through the movements of the stars. This collection provides a wide range of consecutive years of "almanacks" and calendars that depict a vast array of everyday life as it was several hundred years ago.

Early History of Astronomy & Space

Humankind has studied the skies for centuries, seeking to find our place in the universe. Some of the most important discoveries in the field of astronomy were made in these texts recorded by ancient stargazers, but almost as impactful were the perspectives of those who considered their discoveries to be heresy. Any independent astronomer will find this an invaluable collection of titles arguing the truth of the cosmic system.

Early History of Industry & Science

Acting as a kind of historical Wall Street, this collection of industry manuals and records explores the thriving industries of construction; textile, especially wool and linen; salt; livestock; and many more.

Early English Wit, Poetry & Satire

The power of literary device was never more in its prime than during this period of history, where a wide array of political and religious satire mocked the status quo and poetry called humankind to transcend the rigors of daily life through love, God or principle. This series comments on historical patterns of the human condition that are still visible today.

Early English Drama & Theatre

This collection needs no introduction, combining the works of some of the greatest canonical writers of all time, including many plays composed for royalty such as Queen Elizabeth I and King Edward VI. In addition, this series includes history and criticism of drama, as well as examinations of technique.

Early History of Travel & Geography

Offering a fascinating view into the perception of the world during the sixteenth and seventeenth centuries, this collection includes accounts of Columbus's discovery of the Americas and encompasses most of the Age of Discovery, during which Europeans and their descendants intensively explored and mapped the world. This series is a wealth of information from some the most groundbreaking explorers.

Early Fables & Fairy Tales

This series includes many translations, some illustrated, of some of the most well-known mythologies of today, including Aesop's Fables and English fairy tales, as well as many Greek, Latin and even Oriental parables and criticism and interpretation on the subject.

Early Documents of Language & Linguistics

The evolution of English and foreign languages is documented in these original texts studying and recording early philology from the study of a variety of languages including Greek, Latin and Chinese, as well as multilingual volumes, to current slang and obscure words. Translations from Latin, Hebrew and Aramaic, grammar treatises and even dictionaries and guides to translation make this collection rich in cultures from around the world.

Early History of the Law

With extensive collections of land tenure and business law "forms" in Great Britain, this is a comprehensive resource for all kinds of early English legal precedents from feudal to constitutional law, Jewish and Jesuit law, laws about public finance to food supply and forestry, and even "immoral conditions." An abundance of law dictionaries, philosophy and history and criticism completes this series.

Early History of Kings, Queens and Royalty

This collection includes debates on the divine right of kings, royal statutes and proclamations, and political ballads and songs as related to a number of English kings and queens, with notable concentrations on foreign rulers King Louis IX and King Louis XIV of France, and King Philip II of Spain. Writings on ancient rulers and royal tradition focus on Scottish and Roman kings, Cleopatra and the Biblical kings Nebuchadnezzar and Solomon.

Early History of Love, Marriage & Sex

Human relationships intrigued and baffled thinkers and writers well before the postmodern age of psychology and self-help. Now readers can access the insights and intricacies of Anglo-Saxon interactions in sex and love, marriage and politics, and the truth that lies somewhere in between action and thought.

Early History of Medicine, Health & Disease

This series includes fascinating studies on the human brain from as early as the 16th century, as well as early studies on the physiological effects of tobacco use. Anatomy texts, medical treatises and wound treatment are also discussed, revealing the exponential development of medical theory and practice over more than two hundred years.

Early History of Logic, Science and Math

The "hard sciences" developed exponentially during the 16th and 17th centuries, both relying upon centuries of tradition and adding to the foundation of modern application, as is evidenced by this extensive collection. This is a rich collection of practical mathematics as applied to business, carpentry and geography as well as explorations of mathematical instruments and arithmetic; logic and logicians such as Aristotle and Socrates; and a number of scientific disciplines from natural history to physics.

Early History of Military, War and Weaponry

Any professional or amateur student of war will thrill at the untold riches in this collection of war theory and practice in the early Western World. The Age of Discovery and Enlightenment was also a time of great political and religious unrest, revealed in accounts of conflicts such as the Wars of the Roses.

Early History of Food

This collection combines the commercial aspects of food handling, preservation and supply to the more specific aspects of canning and preserving, meat carving, brewing beer and even candy-making with fruits and flowers, with a large resource of cookery and recipe books. Not to be forgotten is a "the great eater of Kent," a study in food habits.

Early History of Religion

From the beginning of recorded history we have looked to the heavens for inspiration and guidance. In these early religious documents, sermons, and pamphlets, we see the spiritual impact on the lives of both royalty and the commoner. We also get insights into a clergy that was growing ever more powerful as a political force. This is one of the world's largest collections of religious works of this type, revealing much about our interpretation of the modern church and spirituality.

Early Social Customs

Social customs, human interaction and leisure are the driving force of any culture. These unique and quirky works give us a glimpse of interesting aspects of day-to-day life as it existed in an earlier time. With books on games, sports, traditions, festivals, and hobbies it is one of the most fascinating collections in the series.

The BiblioLife Network

This project was made possible in part by the BiblioLife Network (BLN), a project aimed at addressing some of the huge challenges facing book preservationists around the world. The BLN includes libraries, library networks, archives, subject matter experts, online communities and library service providers. We believe every book ever published should be available as a high-quality print reproduction; printed on-demand anywhere in the world. This insures the ongoing accessibility of the content and helps generate sustainable revenue for the libraries and organizations that work to preserve these important materials.

The following book is in the "public domain" and represents an authentic reproduction of the text as printed by the original publisher. While we have attempted to accurately maintain the integrity of the original work, there are sometimes problems with the original work or the micro-film from which the books were digitized. This can result in minor errors in reproduction. Possible imperfections include missing and blurred pages, poor pictures, markings and other reproduction issues beyond our control. Because this work is culturally important, we have made it available as part of our commitment to protecting, preserving, and promoting the world's literature.

GUIDE TO FOLD-OUTS MAPS and OVERSIZED IMAGES

The book you are reading was digitized from microfilm captured over the past thirty to forty years. Years after the creation of the original microfilm, the book was converted to digital files and made available in an online database.

In an online database, page images do not need to conform to the size restrictions found in a printed book. When converting these images back into a printed bound book, the page sizes are standardized in ways that maintain the detail of the original. For large images, such as fold-out maps, the original page image is split into two or more pages

Guidelines used to determine how to split the page image follows:

- Some images are split vertically; large images require vertical and horizontal splits.
- For horizontal splits, the content is split left to right.
- For vertical splits, the content is split from top to bottom.
- For both vertical and horizontal splits, the image is processed from top left to bottom right.

THE
Clergyman's Office,
AND THE
Clergyman's Due.

A
SERMON

Preach'd at the *Triennial Visitation* of the Right Reverend
Father in GOD

EDWARD

Lord Bishop of *GLOUCESTER,*
AT
CAMPDEN, *Octob.* 7. 1698.

By *ROBERT MORSE,* A. M. Rector of *Willersy,* in
the County of *Gloucester,* and Master of the *Free-School* in *Campden.*

*Fortis est falsam infamiam contemnere. Sunt qui quod sentiunt, etiamsi
optimum sit, tamen invidiæ metu non audent dicere.* Tul. Of. l. 1. p. 37.

LONDON: Printed for **Tho. Bennet,** at the *Half
Moon* in St. *Paul's Church-Yard,* and **Henry Clements,**
Bookseller, in *Oxford,* 1699.

To the Right Reverend Father in God *Edward*, by Divine Providence, Lord Biſhop of *Glouceſter*.

My Lord,

*H*Aving receiv'd your Lordſhip's Letter to Preach the Viſitation-Sermon at Campden, I was not long in reſolving what Points of Doctrine to inſiſt upon.

The Duty of Prayer took up my Thoughts in the firſt place ; one of the principal Duties of ſinful Men, though now accounted (if we may gueſs by their general Practice) the leaſt of Chriſtian Obligations. I am much afraid, that they who are negligent in coming to the Publick Divine Service, are not more forward in the performance of this indiſpenſible part of Religion elſewhere.

Though Common Prayer is now become a ſcandalous thing in the Opinion of ſome (wo unto them by whom the offence cometh) yet I am perſuaded the more frequent uſe good and wiſe Men make of it, the higher eſteem they muſt have for it.

Diſcourſing once about the Excellency of our Service-Book, (as ſome Men call it by way of contempt, as if Book-Prayer was altogether Antichriſtian) with a Miniſter of the Presbyterian Communion, upon his Accuſations of it in General, I deſir'd him to inſtance in ſome Particular. After ſome pauſe, he at laſt pitch'd upon theſe Words ; Give Peace in our Time, O Lord, becauſe there is none other, &c. God be praiſed, by the Courage and Conduct of His Preſent Majeſty, King William, we have the Bleſſing pray'd for : but, as the Learned

ned

ned Bishop Stillingfleet *says to Mr.* Baxter, *in his excellent Book of the* Unreasonableness of Separation, *on a like occasion; at this rate some Men may want Causes to defend, but they can never want Arguments.*

That I take occasion in the second place to Discourse upon the Duty of Thanksgiving, Gratitude at this time more particularly obliges me, and all of us of the Reform'd Persuasion. For I take it to be past all doubt, that we of the Church of England, and Protestant Religion, were not long since in imminent danger of losing the publick Exercise of it.

In my third and fourth Particulars I aim at the Honour due to the Clergy, upon the account of their Office; and shew that they ought to preserve themselves from Contempt, by a Demeanour suitable to their Sacred Office. That this of ours is a despicable Deanery of Clergy-Men, we dare challenge our greatest Adversaries to prove. Bishop Nicholson us'd to call it his Beloved Deanery; and I hope we shall all deport our selves so as to find the like Approbation in your Lordship, our Diocesan.

That Sober, Religious and Learned Ministers should be any where despis'd, must proceed from a gross and barbarous rudeness of Men, mixt with an Atheistical Genius: Wherever Men have been truly well Bred, sincerely Virtuous and Pious, they have paid their due respects to God's Ministers.

That your Lordship may long enjoy that Happiness, whereever you are concern'd, as you justly merit it by your Love to the Church of England, which among sundry other Instances you have signally demonstrated, in your late Encouragement of the Minister of Cirencester, is the very hearty wish of

    My Lord,
       Your Lordships most Dutiful
          And Humble Servant,

                ROBERT MORSE.

I Theſſal. Chap. V. 17, 18, 19 and 20 Verſes.

Pray without ceaſing: In every thing give thanks, for this is the will of God in Chriſt Jeſus concerning you. Quench not the Spirit: Deſpiſe not Prophecyings.

THE Occaſion of St. *Paul's* Writing this Excellent Epiſtle to the *Theſſalonians*, was the ill uſage thoſe among them who had embraced the Chriſtian Faith received, together with their Apoſtle, who had Preach'd it into their Ears, and by thoſe Inſtruments of Conveyance (God Bleſſing the Seed ſown) by the beſt of Demonſtrations, and moſt Infallible Arguments, rooted it in their Hearts. The hard Treatment they underwent, was from the Unbelieving Jews, or their Adherents, who liv'd in *Theſſalonica*, or were Inhabitants of ſome part or other of *Macedonia*. They were none of them at that diſtance, but their Malice and Revenge would bring them quickly together to Conſult, and effect, if poſſible, the Extirpation of the *Chriſtian Religion*.

The Good Apoſtle had dealt very fairly with theſe Believing *Theſſalonians*, and the other *Macedonian Chriſtians*; he had told them plainly what they muſt truſt to, if they were *Chriſtians* in reality. 'Twas not a Life of Eaſe or Luxury they were to lead, but ſuch as his own; a Life of Labour and hard Travel, yet withal alleviated by a chearful Spirit, and a thankful Commemoration of the Diſciple being like unto his Maſter, and the Servant as his Lord, *Mat.* 10. 25. With an Aſſurance, That Sufferings for Chriſts ſake would not laſt for ever but the recompenee cruelly Tyrannife and Infult over us when they have done : And alfo much Animated they have been to perfift in thefe their Diabolical Attempts, by that victory obtained over Primitive Innocence, whereby their Stratagems have gone on with a more fatal fuccefs over the infirm Pofterity of our Lapfed firft Parents.

2. Befides thefe fierce and implacable Foes, which will always be endeavouring to draw us into Sin, and ruine all our hopes of Eternal Salvation, the World is another Enemy that hath a thoufand Gins to intangle us in ; fuch as, Pride, Ambition, Covetoufnefs, Profanenefs, Irreligion, Voluptuoufnefs, Intemperance, and the like, which if compli'd with, will draw Men into Deftruction and Perdition.

3. Our own corrupt Flefh is apt to concur with thefe, to hinder us from doing good, and incline us to evil ; Hence arife inordinate Affections, and evil Concupifcencies of the Mind. So that we muft needs mifcarry if we rely on our own Strength, and feek not out for fome Affiftance more powerful than our felves ; and how is this to be fought, but from our gracious Father in Heaven, who has promis'd *to be found of them that feek Him*, if they feek him with all their Heart, and with all their Soul. This muft be done by Prayer at the Throne of Grace ; and to this end the Apoftle tells us, *that we muft pray always with all prayer and fupplication in the Spirit, and watch thereunto with all perfeverance*, Eph. 6. 18. This he had from our Saviour, who commands us to *watch and pray left we enter into temptation*; Mat. 26. 41. and *always to pray and not to faint*, Luke 18. 1. We *muft pray every where*, faith St. *Paul, lifting up holy hands, without wrath and doubting*, 1 Tim. 2. 8.

By this Prayer to God's Majefty, as we are taught to ufe it, we diftinguifh our felves from Atheifts and Heathens ;

thens; Tis true the Heathens themselves, by the Dictates of natural Reason and Religion, held themselves obliged to one fort of Adoration or another; but here was the mischief, their Gods were no Gods; they Worshipped the Fond Imaginations of their own Hearts, and many times the work of their own Hands. They carved themselves Gods out of some senseless Stone, or hewed them out of some inanimate Tree; of part

Mentis ludicras omnia.
Pictâ ludibria trunci.
Autebur in varias aut saxa incisa figuras.

whereof they made them a Fire to warm their Hands at; of the other part they fashioned them Gods to invoke and hold up their Hands unto. To this *Horace* alludes, *Serm. Lib.* 1. *Sat.* 8.

Olim Truncus eram ficulnus, inutile lignum,
Cum faber incertis fcamnum faceret ne Priapum
Maluit esse Deum.

But our Addresses are to the right Object, and Owner, God alone; A God that can hear our Prayers, and not only can but will; a God that takes pleasure in our Applications to him, and hath commanded us not to neglect it to our own hurt. We continually stand in need of God's Forgiveness and Pardon; when we have Sinned (as, alas! who is there that Sins not?) we must pray for the averting God's Wrath and Indignation; we cannot be penitent if we pray not; if we confess not our Sins, we must not expect an Absolution of them.

Neither is the whole Duty of Prayer consisting of Confession alone, to expiate for the past Offences of our Lives; but tis also necessary to be used as a Method of Prevention for the time to come. This is the Antidote to keep off the infection of all Spiritual Maladies, the omission whereof is like going out fasting in a time of Epedi-

mical

duce to a Pious Chriſtian, when for want of Time, he can uſe no longer Addreſs: what Comfort it brings to an humble Penitent, though he ſay no more but with the Poor *Publican* in the Goſpel, ſmiting his Breaſt, *God be Merciful to me a Sinner.* Morning and Evening we ſhould implore God's Pardon for our Iniquities, his Grace to Support us, and Enable us to ſerve Him; but as for Ejaculations, they ſhould be as frequent, I had almoſt ſaid, as our Pulſe beats, as the Minutes of our dying Breath.

2. Family-Devotions ſhould not, unleſs upon very extraordinary Occaſions, be paſſed by Morning and Evening; that ſo we may make a neat Epitome of the Church of G O D, in our ſeveral Habitations. Then,

3. As for Common-Prayers, or the Prayers of the Church, they are the beſt of all, eſpecially as we have them; and we ſhould be preſent at them, without ceaſing, as my Text ſays, ἀδιαλείπτως, without leaving off; not forſaking the Aſſembling of our ſelves together for this purpoſe. They are the Publick Prayers of the Church, as Expoſitors tells us, that St. *Paul* chiefly means in this place, ἐν παντὶ καιρῷ. The Words are (St. *Luke,* Chap. 21. and Ver. 26.) *Always,* that is upon all Opportunities, eſpecially upon the *Lord's Day,* and other Feaſts and Faſts of the Church.

And however it may be allowed us at home, to uſe a greater and more unconfin'd Freedom of Expreſſion, by our ſelves, or with our Families in ſome particular caſes; (though there I think Forms, generally ſpeaking, moſt proper to be obſerv'd) yet for the Church of God, I eſteem Forms of Prayer, and an Eſtabliſhed Liturgy, ſo far from Stinting of the Spirit (as some Men would have it, who know not what they mean, or else would not have other poor ignorant Wretches understand) that nothing but wild Disorder and Confusion would arise amongst us, if every one (who only fancies himself sufficient for the Work) was to be his own, and the Congregations Prayer-Maker, upon every Return of Divine Worship, who knows not how to Pray with the Spirit, and to Pray with the Understanding also, 1 *Cor.* chap. 14. ver. 15.

And this may suffice for the Duty of Prayer. Only let me add this, with all humble Submission to you (my Reverend and Learned Brethren of the Clergy) to beseech you still to use the Prayers of the Church, with such Decency and Devotion, as may shew you to have truly Pious, and well-affected Souls; and that you Love and Admire the Unparallel'd Prayers of the Church, beyond any other Compositions whatsoever: And as for the Crude, Extempore Effusions of Enthusiasts, that you esteem them to admit of no Comparison (but what is odious) with them.

Secondly, I pass on now to the Duty of Thanksgiving, and the Universality thereof, and for what reason; of which more briefly.

The Apostle tells us, *We must in every thing give thanks, because this is the will of God in Christ Jesus concerning us.* Which is as much as to say, That we must look unto God, as the great Disposer of all the things of this World, and that what He allots, is best for us, in General and in Particular. If He ordains us Adversities, Troubles and

Sick-

Sickneſſes, Patience and Submiſſion will carry us through them, when Murmuring and Diſcontent will not eaſe our Load here, but aggravate that and our Guilt together; and Repining and Reluctance under our preſent Infelicities, will but conſign us to a more irreverſible State of Diſſatisfaction hereafter. The Apoſtle tells his *Theſſalonians*, That this is the will of God, that they ſhould in every thing give Thanks, even in Tribulations and Afflictions for the ſake of Chriſt Jeſus, whoſe Diſciples they were. *Rejoice evermore*, ſays he, *ver.* 16. of this Chapter.

Now this is the Life of our Religion in all Occurrences, to be of a Thankful Temper to our good God, and to Adore him for his unſpeakable Gifts, the Gifts of Food and Rayment, Health, Relations, Friends and Benefactors; all the Neceſſaries and Conveniencies of this Life; but above all for the means of Grace and hopes of Glory; for the Purity of the Reformed Religion, and the Benefits of the Goſpel Light, which we enjoy in this our *Goſhen*. That we are not overwhelmed by the Darkneſs of *Popiſh Superſtition*, by thoſe ſundry and late Attempts that have been made to bereave us of this Happineſs; that we are not deprived of the Ineſtimable Priviledge of ſerving God in ſuch conſecrated Places as this, after the beſt and moſt Primitive Modes of Worſhip; that the unjuſtifiable Paradoxes either of *Rome* or *Geneva* are not Tranſplanted hither: We ought to render thanks, both Miniſters and People, not only with our Lips, but in our Lives. And that will induce God, when he ſees us thus greateful to him, to continue us in the ſtate we are now, Objects of his Divine Favour, in the preſervation of our Church, as it is now amongſt us Eſtabliſhed, bleſſed be his wonderful and moſt Glorious Goodneſs for it.

All

All you of our Communion, ought in particular to confider your Felicity in being within the Pale of the Church, and that you have not blind Guides to lead you aftray, you know not whither, till you fall into the Bottom- lefs Pit; that you have fuch for your Paftors, as are able to confute all Gainfayers, able and willing to inftruct you in all the neceffary Points of Salvation, rightly divid- ing the word of God, and not rending it afunder, as the manner of fome is; fuch as Pray for you without ceafing, at home and in the Church; fuch as inftruct your Children in the Fundamentals of Chriftianity; the Excel- lent Church Catechifm; and your felves, as well as them, in the Expofition of it; fuch as vifit you in all your Diftreffes, and Trials, councel, comfort, fuccour you; For thefe Bleffings we ought all to give Thanks, and for the enjoyments of the Gofpel without the cruelties of an Inquifition, or the barbarities of an Oliverian fequeftration. For if the *Theffalonians* were in every thing to give thanks, and rejoyce in the Lord always, tho. furrounded with Perfecutions, much more we who have no difturbance in our Religion, as the poor Afflicted Proteftants now in *France* and *Savoy*, and other places have, whom God of his All-fufficient Grace fupport, God of his Infinite Good- nefs in his due time deliver.

3. I proceed now, after thefe two foregoing pofitive precepts, to one that is negative, which is this, *Quench not the Spirit*, including, as I intimated, this affirmative, *viz.* That we reverence the real Gifts of Good and Faithful Minifters, Sound and Orthodox Divines. The Spirit of God does not now adays Operate in an extraodinary man- ner, as in the Primitive Times, fo as to ennable Men, other- wife Illiterate, as moft of the Apoftles were, to fpeak divers Languages, not taught them the common way.

The

The Apoftles were ꭲꞷ꭮꭯ꞷ꭯ꞇ꭮Θ, Infpired by the Holy Ghoft, and in a more peculiar manner ꞷꞇꞷꞇ꭮꭮꭮꭮꭮꭮, Taught Immediately by God. The holy Ghoft defcended vifibly, in Cloven Tongues, like as of Fire, as appears from *Acts*, Second and Third, from whence this paffage of *not Quenching the Spirit*, feems to be deriv'd. And to Give them their due, tho' many Enthufiafts boaft of Infpiration, Extraordinary Call, and Apoftolical Endowments, to qualify them for the Work of the Miniftery, they pretend not to the Gift of Tongues ; here they will grant that the Spirit is ftinted to them, and that they are not abfolutely fo good Linguifts as the Apoftles were.

They have had thofe among them indeed, who have made a vain Oftentation of this gift alfo ; but they have been Subtile Popifh Priefts in Mafquerade, who in Mechanical Dreffes, have endeavoured to make men believe, that they never had any learned Education, and yet that they did not want it, as having no lefs a Perfon than the Holy Ghoft himfelf for their Tutor, who has taught them the Learned Tongues ; but thefe have been detected for Impoftors, by trying them in fuch Languages as they have not underftood. And fo for the gift of Healing, Curing the Deaf, Blind, Dumb, Lunatick and Paralytick, and Ejecting of Devils, they do not lay claim to them ; and yet one thing, obferve by the way, they affume to themfelves, which is the Gift of Unpremeditated Prayer, and yet that is not mentioned amongft any of the Gifts of the Holy Ghoft, defcribed at large in 1 *Cor.* 12. nor in any other place of Holy Scripture befide.

It may be asked then here, What is the Quenching of the Spirit now adays ? Doth not the Spirit of God work ftill on the Children of Obedience, as well as the Evil Spirit on the Children of Difobedience ? *Eph.* 2. 2.

I An-

I Anſwer Yes, without doubt, ſo as to aſſiſt all thoſe that uſe honeſt Endeavours, and proper Means, to fit themſelves for the Miniſterial Function. But how can we once think that God will work Miracles upon ſome, to ſave them the Pains of Study, and the Charges of Education, and forſake others, that by all poſſible care, have made it their Buſineſs, and been at great Expence both of Time, and upon other accounts, to qualiſie themſelves for the Embaſſadors of Chriſt Jeſus, 2 *Cor.* 5. 20.

For my part (and I doubt not the concurrent Sentiments of all unprejudic'd and conſiderate Perſons) I give no credit to any that arrogate to themſelves a Supernatural Call to the Miniſtry. With great and profound Humility, we Sons of the Church of *England,* are ready to acknowledge, That the beſt Men of us all are unable to act any good thing, as of our ſelves alone, but our Sufficiency is of God. We owe all we can ſay or do well, to the Aid of God's good and gracious Spirit, Co-operating with our earneſt tho' weak Endeavours. But how unlikely is it, and indeed abſurd, to imagine, That God ſhould deny us the Bleſſings of his Holy Spirit, who are always praying for its Sanctifying Influences, kind and benign Aſſiſtances, and by inceſſant Studies, ſtriving to improve our Talents of Grace, Learning and Knowledge, for the Edification of our Brethren; and beſtow it in a Super-eminent degree upon Perſons who never had any extraordinary Parts, or common Ingenious Education, ſo as to enable them to do more without any precious Pains, than thoſe who have always been diligent to ſupply themſelves with neceſſary Sciences of all ſorts, in order to the great Work of the Miniſtry?

Certainly our Heavenly Father hath always been more propitious to the ſedulous Endeavours of his Pious Servant, joyning the help of his Spirit with ordinary means; ſuch as Learning, Study, Meditation, comparing of Paſ-

ſages

ſages of Holy Scripture one with another, Conſulting *Original Languages*, and the like. This undoubtedly is the way to a true Goſpel-Miniſtry, to have ſuch for the Guide of Souls, as have had good Education, have been ſuch Studious Preparers of themſelves for their Sacred Office, that as it would be preſumption in them in the higheſt degree, to expect Miracles in theſe Days, to make them Learned *Rabbins extempore* of Illiterate Men, ſo (God be praiſed) it is no wiſe neceſſary for them to plead any ſuch thing, as being qualify'd for the Work in the uſual Method, as the Nature of our Eſtabliſh'd Church requires, *viz.* by being taught the Learned Tongues in their youthful Days, Philoſophical Inſtitutions in their freſher Academick Gowns (which Philoſophy is juſtly Stiled the *Hand-maid to Divinity*) and afterward in the Maturity of their Judgments, have ſearched into the great Truths of the *Chriſtian Religion*, Peruſed the Councils, Fathers and Primitive Writers, and the Defences and Apologies of our Church, againſt all ſorts of Oppoſers. Which by the Grace of God will ſtill be done, againſt *Atheiſts* and *Theiſts*, which, I look upon to be as near in their Notions, as they are in their Names, if not, many of them (though diſſembled) altogether the ſame: Againſt *Socinians*, who deny the Lord that bought them, and put him to an open ſhame, who, as far as in them lies, make Him ſuffer in his Divinity, as he did once in his Humanity: Againſt *Jeſuited Romaniſts*, and Bigotted Separatiſts and Schiſmaticks, of what Denomination whatſoever; in the mean time ſhewing a Spirit of Moderation, and of ſome having Compaſſion, making a difference, as St. *Jude* ſpeaks, *ver.* 22. endeavouring to win them, together with the Strength of Arguments, by all the Sweetneſs of Temper imaginable, Brotherly Love and Reſpect, Neighbourly Viſits, eſpecially in any Affliction, extraordinary Emergency

gency or Occafion; but above all, by the Gravity of our Deportment, and the Luftre and Ornament of Sober and Religious Lives.

Where there is fuch a Miniftry, as God be thanked ours is, And Honour is due; Divines that have been Epifcopally Ordain'd, according to the cuftom of the Church from the Apoftles times, having been ftrictly examined as to their Abilities before admitted Graduates in the Univerfities; afterward, before the Impofition of Hands for the Sufception of Holy Orders, by the Holy Prelates of the Church themfelves, or by perfons of Learning and Integrity deputed by them, whom they can fafely confide in for that weighty purpofe.

Thefe are the Levites that (as the Scripture fpeaks) the Laity are not to forfake as long as they live upon the earth, *Deut.* 12. 19. fuch are to be reverenc'd for their works fake, the Meffage which they came upon, being no lefs than the Reconciliation of Men to God; the Salvation of their unvaluable and immortal Souls. Which is one great meaning of the *not quenching the Spirit*; that as the Minifters of the Gofpel fhould not by neglect of their Office, and illnefs of their lifes (which God avert) drive off the Holy Spirit from affifting them in their Labours, but keep up Godlinefs and Religion, by devout Prayer and good Preaching, joyned with a fober exemplary Life and Converfation; fo where fuch perfons and gifts are feen, none fhould be averfe to them, as if they were falfe Prophets; None fhould rob them of their Tithes and Dues, which is call'd *robbing of God*, *Malac.* the 3*d*. and *v*. 8. and fuch facriligious Perfons are faid to be *curfed with a Curfe* in the verfe following; None fhould wrong them in their good Names, by execrable Lies and Villainous Slanders, or any way grieve or mifufe them; none fhould be *morimexul* (as I may fo fpeak) *haters of the Clergy*, which

which yet more than a good many are, but φιλοκληρικοι, *lovers of the Clergy*, remembring that antient observation, *Qui vera fide colit Deum, amat etiam Sacerdotum.* He that loveth God in sincerity, loves his Ministers so too; and as the Apostle speaks, *let us be so accounted of, as Ministers of Christ, and stewards of the Mysteries of God.* 1 Cor. 4. 1. And that all we that are Ministers of Christ, and Stewards of the Mysteries of God, may be found faithful in our several Stations, which is required of us *v.* 2 of that Chapter. May the Good Spirit of God guide and direct us, that thus by the goodness of our Lives, and soundness of our Doctrine, we may save both our selves and them that hear us, 1 *Tim.* 4. 16.

4. Which introduces the *Fourth and last* Particular, *Despise not Prophecying, i. e.* Genuine Interpretations of the Word of God, the Holy Scriptures, nor consequently those that make them, *such as labour in the Word and Doctrine,* as the Apostle's expression is to *Timothy,* 1 *Tim.* 5. 17.

The Holy Scripture is the Rule that we are all to walk by, and the Expounding of this, and the exciting our Brethren, from the Examples, Precepts, Promises, and Threats thereof, how to deport themselves, is our Ministerial Office and Duty. That the word *Prophecy is Interpreting Scripture* and preaching upon it, is evident from the 14 *Chap.* of the 1 *Ep.* to the *Cor. v.* 1. *Follow after Charity, and desire spiritual gifts, but rather that ye may prophecy*; and *v.* 3. 4. He that Prophecieth, speaketh unto men to Edification, and Exhortation and Comfort; he that speaketh in an unknown Tongue, edifieth himself, but he that prophecieth Edifieth the Church. This was our Saviour Christ's Prophetick Office, to make known the Will of God to the World, and so all that have in any good degree done the like, are stiled *Prophets,* all that have Taught men their Duty towards God and man. Thus

among

among the *Pagans*, the Divines who taught them what
they ought to do, their Priests or Religious Persons,
were termed *Vates*, Prophets. The word doth always
imply such as are indu'd with a Spirit of foretelling *future
Events*, but as *Grammarians*, informs us, naturally signifies no more than a *Procurator*, or *Prolocutor*, speaking from,
or instead of another, or acting in his stead ; as a *Pro-
Consul* is he that supplies the *Consul's* Place, προ in Com-
position being the same with ὑπέρ. Upon this account the
Jewish High-Priest was a Prophet to his People, who en-
tring into the *Sanctum Sanctorum*, the Holy of Holies, to
inform himself of God's Will, was to reveal the same to
the People. In the like Sense it is that God saith to *Mo-
ses*, concerning *Aaron*, *He shall be thy Spokesman to the
People, and he shall be to thee a mouth, and thou shalt be to
him instead of God*, Exod. 4. 16. That which is here
render'd *Spokesman, Orator, or Prolocutor*, is Chap. 7. 5.
Interpreted Prophet. *See* (saith God) *I have made thee a
God to Pharaoh, and Aaron thy brother shall be thy Prophet*.
In the acceptation of speaking from Man to God, *Abra-
ham* is call'd a Prophet, *Gen.* 20. v. 7. where God in a
Dream speaketh to *Abimilech* in this manner : *Now there-
fore restore the man his wife, for he is a Prophet, and he shall
pray for thee*. Whence may be inferr'd, that the Appella-
tion of *Prophet* may be ascribed, not improperly, to them
who in *Christian Congregations* have a due *Ministerial Call*
to put up publick Petitions for their People, and Admi-
nister all the Offices of Religious Worship. Now, though
the Word of God it self, in this degenerate Age, is despised
by many evil Men, under the Notion of Reveal'd Religion, which they are great Contemners of, yet since it is
clear as the Sun, that it is unjustly and groundless (no
Writings whatsoever having the like Authentick Truth,
as the Learned Bishop *Stillingfleet*, in his *Origines Sacra*,

makes

makes appear) So I take those Words to be Reflection sufficient upon them, and which ought to be a Terror to them, from the Examples of others, as being spoken on the like occasion, *Acts* 13. 41. *Behold the despisers, and wonder, and perish.* The Despisers of the Gospel are here particularly threatned, for disbelieving and rejecting our Saviour's Resurrection, and other Divine Works fore-told by the Prophets long before. And what if the *Romanists* vilifie this Word of God in comparison with their Traditions, their Foolish and Ridiculous Legends (as the *Pharisees* of old) is it ever the worse in it self? No, 'tis for this very reason that they do it, assign'd by St. *John*, chap. 3. 20. *Every one that doth evil hateth the light, neither cometh to the light, lest his deeds should be reproved.* And as for those that call it a *Dead Letter*, doubt we not, upon the good evidence we have, but they receiv'd it from those Deluders, the first Projectors of this rude and ill manner'd antick and ridiculous Profession.

As to us Ministers of the Church of *England*, we desire upon all accounts to have the Scripture for our Test, *To the Law and to the Testimony*, as *Isaiah* speaks, *Isa.* 8. 20. *They who speak not according to this word, it is because there is no light in them.* If the Scripture be not on our side, let none bid us *God speed*, or wish us good luck in the Name of the Lord, 2 *John* 10. *Maledictus est*, saith St. *Austin, qui quidpiam prædicat, præterquam, quod in Scripturis legis & Evangelii recepimus. Though an Angel from Heaven should preach otherwise, let him be ascursed,* Gal. 1. 8. But (as it hath been sufficiently prov'd against all our Adversaries) if we act consonantly to the Word of God, derive the Authority of our Commission and Doctrine from thence, and live accordingly, then are we not to be despised, *but to be accounted worthy of a double Honour ; then they that despise us, despise Christ that sent us, and our Heavenly Father that sent Him,*

Him; Luk. 10. 19. *Despise not man but God, who hath given unto us his holy Spirit,* 1 Thes. 4. 8.

St. *Paul* tells us, 2 Tim. 3. *That the Scriptures are able to make us wise unto Salvation, through Faith which is in Christ Jesus: And that all Scripture is given by Inspiration of God, and is profitable for doctrine, for reproof, for correction, for instruction in righteousness, that the man of God may be perfect, throughly furnished unto all good works.* ὁ τοῦ Θεοῦ ἄνθρωπος, The Man of God, that is the Teacher or Preacher of the Gospel, sent, and authorised by God, may by the Study of the Scriptures be supply'd upon all Occasions to discharge his Duty towards Men's precious Souls, committed to his care.

The necessity of these publick Instructions from the Publick, may be deduc'd from *Rom.* 10. 14, 15. *How shall they call on him, on whom they have not believ'd? And how shall they believe in Him, of whom they have not heard? And how shall they hear without a Preacher? And how shall they preach except they be sent? As it is written, How beautiful are the feet of them that preach the Gospel of Peace, and bring glad tydings of good things?*

That the Ministers of our Church are lawfully Commissioned, and sent to Preach the Gospel, I have shewed before, as not usurping the Office of the Ministery, but having receiv'd the Laying on of the Hands of the Presbytery, πρεσβυτερίε, the Bishops, as the Word signifies; no Inferiour Novel Imposition.

Which Episcopal Order, that it hath been from the Apostles times, is manifest from the Apostles themselves: For St. *Peter* was Bishop of *Antioch*; *Titus* Arch-Bishop of *Crete*, and *Timothy* Bishop of *Ephesus.* And we need go no further for the proof of it, than those Words in this Chapter, *Ver.* 12. & 3. where you find my Text; *We beseech you Brethren, to know them which labour among you,*

and

and are over you in the Lord, and admonish you, and to esteem them very highly in Love for their works sake. The *Greek* Words, περιςάμενοι ὑμῶν, *those are set, or rule over you,* signifie the Bishops of the several Churches in those days, call'd in the first times περιςᾶτις, as the Learned Dr. *Hammond* observes. As appears then, Preaching was one of the Bishop's principal Works of old, which since they cannot do so constantly in all places now adays, their Dioceffes being so large, and their Avocations so frequent upon diverse accounts, our Church has found it neceffary to have settled Parochial Ministers, who are to be Faithful and Wife Stewards under Christ and them, Rectors or Rulers over God's Houshold, the Church, to give them their Portion of Meat, Spiritual Sustenance for their Souls, in due Season.

To conclude then, Happy ye Sons of the Tribe of *Levi,* the Lot of God's own Inheritance, Priests of the Most High God ; who like *Timothy,* from your Youth have Study'd the Word of God, and ever since made it your Employment and Delight together, to Consult these Lively Oracles : Here is the inexhaustible Fountain of Comfort, to which you Shepherds of Souls are to lead your Flocks ; here are the Pastures whence you are to Feed those whom Christ hath Purchased with his own Blood ; from this Magazine you are to Arm your selves and others, to *war a good warfare ; fight the good fight of faith, and lay hold on eternal life :* Hence you are to supply your selves with Materials, as the Apostle speaks in this Chapter, *v.* 14. where my Text is, *To warn them that are unruly, comfort the feeble-minded, support the weak, and be patient towards all men ;* i. e. To preserve your Flocks from the Inroads of Wolves in Sheeps clothing, to spare no Pains to reduce the lost or straggling Sheep, from the Example of the good Shepherd in the Gospel, *That bore him on his shoulders rejoicing,*

joicing, Luke 15. 5. Hence, like *Boanerges*, the Sons of Thunder, whilst you proclaim the Terrors of the Lord against hardned and presumptuous Sinners, you are to Animate the timerous and weak of Faith, that they despair not, pouring Oil into their Wounds, and shewing them what a Gracious God, upon unfeigned Repentance, they have to deal with. And as the Apostle speaks to the *Galatians*, *Gal.* 6. 1. to restore such as are overtaken in a. Fault. *Brethren*, says he, *if a man be overtaken in a fault, ye which are spiritual*, πνδματικοὶ, Divines, *restore such a one in the spirit of meekness*. Blessed are they, whom the Lord, when he cometh, shall find so doing; if He come in the *Second*, or come in the *Third Watch*, blessed are those Servants; assuredly, when Christ, the Chief Shepherd shall appear, they shall receive a Crown of Glory that fadeth. not away.

F I N I S.

CPSIA information can be obtained at www.ICGtesting.com
Printed in the USA
BVOW09s1019111115

426698BV00019B/296/P

9 781240 855537